COCKATIELS
KW-057

Contents

Photographers: Dr. Gerald R. Allen, Glen S. Axelrod, Dr. Herbert R. Axelrod, H. Bielfeld, E. Goldfinger, Isabelle Francais, Michael Gilroy, Jack Harris, B. Kahl, Harry V. Lacey, Bruce D. Lavoy, P. Leysen, J. Maier, R. and V. Moat, Fritz Prenzel, Nancy Richmond, San Diego Zoo, Brian Seed, Vince Serbin, Vogelpark Walsrode, Dr. Matthew M. Vriends.

Overleaf: A lovely lutino cockatiel. **Title page:** A normal gray cockatiel and a pied cockatiel.

Distributed in the UNITED STATES by T.F.H. Publications, Inc., One T.F.H. Plaza, Neptune City, NJ 07753; in CANADA to the Pet Trade by H & L Pet Supplies Inc., 27 Kingston Crescent, Kitchener, Ontario N2B 2T6; Rolf C. Hagen Ltd., 3225 Sartelon Street, Montreal 382 Quebec; in CANADA to the Book Trade by Macmillan of Canada (A Division of Canada Publishing Corporation), 164 Commander Boulevard, Agincourt, Ontario M1S 3C7; in ENGLAND by T.F.H. Publications Limited, Cliveden House/Priors Way/Bray, Maidenhead, Berkshire SL6 2HP, England; in AUSTRALIA AND THE SOUTH PACIFIC by T.F.H. (Australia) Pty. Ltd., Box 149, Brookvale 2100 N.S.W., Australia; in NEW ZEALAND by Ross Haines & Son, Ltd., 18 Monmouth Street, Grey Lynn, Auckland 2, New Zealand; in SINGAPORE AND MALAYSIA by MPH Distributors (S) Pte., Ltd., 601 Sims Drive, #03/07/21, Singapore 1438; in the PHILIPPINES by Bio-Research, 5 Lippay Street, San Lorenzo Village, Makati Rizal; in SOUTH AFRICA by Multipet Pty. Ltd., 30 Turners Avenue, Durban 4001. Published by T.F.H. Publications, Inc. Manufactured in the United States of America by T.F.H. Publications, Inc.

COCKATIELS

LAURA TARTAK

Left: *The cockatiel is the only species of its genus; some aviculturists say that this genus is the connecting link between parrots and cockatoos. This bird is a wild cockatiel.* Below: *The lutino cockatiel is one of the oldest cockatiel mutations.*

Introduction

Of the many parrots and parrotlike birds that are available today, the cockatiel appears to be the ideal pet parrot. In popularity it occupies a position between the very popular budgerigar (best known in the United States as a parakeet) and the very exotic and larger parrots (macaws, cockatoos, etc.). It is true that there are some parrots of the same size as the cockatiel that are often more colorful, but

such birds are not as easily available nor as well known in their habits.

An apartment dweller who does not have much space to spare and has neighbors to consider but wants to have a pet parrot can choose a cockatiel. The cockatiel is easy to tame, its cage would take up very little space, and its voice is not raucous and irritating.

Cockatiels are relatively inexpensive in comparison to other parrots and yet are not so commonplace as budgies.

It will not be difficult to get a pair of cockatiels; the sexes are distinct externally. Both sexes are capable of talking, although males seem to have a greater aptitude for talking than females. Cockatiels can even whistle and imitate tunes.

These gregarious birds get along with other small species of parrots, budgerigars, finches, etc, and they have a relatively long life span (about 15 to 20 years or more in captivity).

A pair of normal gray cockatiels. Cockatiels are the most inexpensive parrots on the market, and they are usually available in most pet shops.

Headstudy of a normal gray cockatiel. Cockatiels have a life span of 15 to 20 years, and most birds in captivity live longer than their wild counterparts.

THE WILD COCKATIEL

At present the cockatiel is scientifically known as *Nymphicus hollandicus.* Modern taxonomists or systematists (qualified scientific classifiers) are not agreed as to the exact position of the cockatiel in relation to other parrots. However, it is a very distinct species and it deserves its own genus (species group). Some taxonomists and behaviorists align it with the cockatoos in a separate family (Cacatuidae), while others are of the opinion that all these birds are members of a very large parrot family (Psittacidae).

The cockatiel, as its scientific name indicates, was first

Cockatiels are considered to be one of the most free-breeding species of parrots. Their general breeding management is similar to that of the budgerigar. **Opposite:** Birds bred frequently in captivity over a long period of time usually produce a number of different color varieties. This bird is a pearled cockatiel. **Right:** A lutino cockatiel. **Below:** A trio of normal gray cockatiels.

discovered in eastern Australia (Australia was then known as New Holland). Cockatiels were reported by the naturalists who sailed with Captain Cook on his voyage to eastern Australia in 1770. They were described and published later in a manner not acceptable to modern methods of nomenclature. Although the bird had been cited in early books under different names, it received its present name in 1832, when the genus *Nymphicus* was suggested by Wagler.

As communications and travel improved between the colonies and Great Britain, scientists collected specimens for their museums, and naturalists were able to describe the habitat of the cockatiel. Through these expeditions, several specimens were brought into England and Europe.

The cockatiel species is distributed through the Australian continent but is absent from Tasmania. The systematic history (synonymy) of the cockatiel indicates that some taxonomists see differences present in populations from different areas of Australia.

Nevertheless, according to most scientists, these differences are not enough to justify splitting the species into various subspecies.

In the wild, cockatiels, according to the great British naturalist John Gould, are more numerous in the eastern than in the western regions of Australia. His observations were made about the middle of the last century. He reported that large numbers of cockatiels (known to him as cockatoo parrakeets) cover the ground while feeding. They are found in groups, seem to prefer dead branches of trees, are capable of sustained flight, and frequent areas close to streams. Cockatiels are not timid birds and, since they are considered good for eating, many are killed by the natives.

The wild cockatiel inhabits much of Australia, particularly the drier inlands away from the coastal regions. These birds are found near water sites

Opposite: *Artist's rendering of a wild, normal gray cockatiel. Cockatiels are gregarious birds that will seldom live apart from their flock.*

Opposite: *The white cockatiel is a domestically bred bird; its color is sex-linked in its manner of inheritance. Breeders continue to strive for a very white bird.* **Above:** *A wild cockatiel feeding on leaves.* **Right:** *A typical wild cockatiel habitat in Australia.*

such as rivers, streams and creeks, and their movements are controlled by the availability of a water supply.

Cockatiels seem to favor the eastern or western parts of Australia as breeding grounds. Each year a considerable number of pairs gather in the wooded areas adjacent to rivers and streams. An etching of these cockatiels resting by a creek appears in *Cassell's Book of Birds*. These birds usually prefer to make their nests in holes, hollow branches, or in decaying stumps of dead trees; only necessity will coerce them into nesting in live trees. Wild cockatiels lay their eggs on a bed of decayed wood or on chippings that are on the bottom of a scooped out saucer-shaped depression made in their nesting hole. No nesting materials are used. The eggs are white and oval-shaped, and clutch size varies from three to ten, according to the maturity of the birds and the time of year.

Cockatiels enjoy companionship, whether it is that of other birds or of humans. They should, however, be given adequate time to adjust to any new acquaintances.

A pied cockatiel. In the wild, cockatiels are often ground eaters that live mostly on vegetation.

These cockatiels feed on seeds of many grasses and herbage, leaves and bark from plants, and bushes and trees that grow on the vast Australian plains. Seasonal grubs and insects are also consumed by these ground eaters.

Wild cockatiels are usually tolerant of human beings, so it is not unusual to find them in gardens and parks of built-up areas. If a cockatiel is frightened by a sudden movement, it will simply fly to a nearby tree and remain there until the human disturbance passes by. Being gregarious, they travel from site to site in numbers; it is rare to find a solitary wild cockatiel.

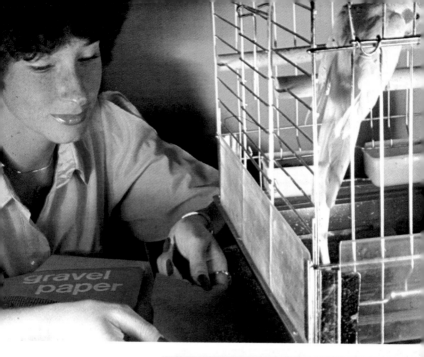

Opposite top: *Cockatiels need some sort of gravel mixture in their cage, as it is an important source of minerals. A selection of gravel paper and other accessories can be found in your local pet shop.* **Opposite bottom:** *Preparing the gravel paper for placement in the cage.* **Above:** *Placing the paper on the bottom of the cage.* **Right:** *Grit being placed loosely on the bottom of the cage. Most breeders believe it is more desirable to keep a separate vessel for the grit.*

Housing

Cockatiels are approximately 13 inches long and should be housed in similar but larger structures than budgerigars or canaries. Wooden or all-wire parrot cages (square or round) make good homes for single pet cockatiels. Breeding pairs are often housed in large cages, pens, indoor aviaries, and flighted or unflighted garden aviaries, depending upon the breeder's space availability. For exhibition purposes, large stock cages are needed for the bird's initial training. Budgerigars, finch-like species, and most cockatiels of all colors are very friendly toward one another and consequently make ideal inmates for a large or small collection of mixed aviary housing.

Cockatiels do not fly as much or as frequently as other smaller parrot species; nevertheless, they do require a reasonable amount of flying and exercise room if they are to remain in a healthy, fit, vigorous condition.

Most breeders find that cockatiels reproduce at their greatest capacity when housed in aviaries, particularly those with access to an outside flight. The size of the flight should be about twice the length of the sleeping quarters. If the sleeping area were 6½ feet long, then the flight should be approximately 13 feet in length. The actual size of an aviary is controlled by the amount of available space and the number of birds kept by the breeder. The density of a colony population may be greater than other parakeets since cockatiels are so amenable. Breeders, though, should realize that overcrowding an aviary is undesirable if successful breeding results are to be obtained.

Cockatiels are gnawers; they quickly kill growing shrubs and any other living plants placed in their cages. Grasses of various kinds can be grown successfully on the floor of a flight to provide green food and a playground for the birds. Perches must be placed in the flight to give the birds an opportunity to gnaw. If

Opposite: *A beautiful normal gray cockatiel perching atop its cage. Metal cages are usually preferable to wooden ones, as cockatiels, being gnawers, are capable of damaging their all-wood homes.*

Left: *Regardless of how attentive you are to your pet's dietary needs, it is a good idea to add a quality vitamin-mineral supplement to your cockatiel's food.* **Below:** *Cockatiels, like most parrots, are avid chewers. Any wood placed in their living quarters will soon be chewed to pieces.* **Opposite top and bottom:** *All water and seed that is given to the cockatiel must be fresh and clean.*

possible, the perches should be made from branches of fruit, hazelnut, willow, alder, elm, hawthorn, sloe, or similar trees. Machine dowelling may be used if the breeder cannot obtain natural perches. Small twigs from safe trees (those that have never been treated with chemicals) should be given to cockatiels. These birds need certain amounts of green food, especially during the breeding periods. In addition, by supplying these birds with this extra gnawing material, the risk of damaging the aviary's wooden parts is reduced. The breeder needs to periodically renew all types of perching. If the perches are not firmly fixed, mating may not be successful and eggs will then be clear or infertile. Cockatiel perches should be considerably greater in diameter than those of a budgerigar or canary.

A wide range of materials can be used to build new

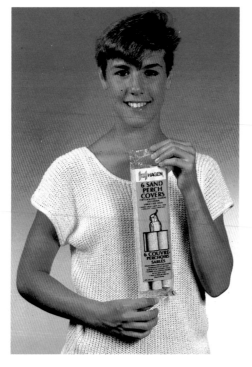

Some owners like to use sand perch covers, which are available in pet shops. However, if safe natural branches are available for frequent use, your birds may not need help in wearing down their claws.

The perch is an essential element of the cockatiel cage; there must be enough perches available for all birds kept together.

aviaries suitable for keeping and breeding cockatiels. Various kinds of existing buildings can easily be adapted for the same purposes. The breeder must first decide whether he wants colony or single pair (controlled) breeding. It is advisable to find out from the local government if there are any regulations concerning building a garden aviary. Urban areas are usually zoned as to what types of structures can be built.

If a breeder has chosen to aim for serious color production, then the single pair method must be employed to have complete control over each breeding pair. One breeding pair to a compartment is the only way pedigrees may be guaranteed. Cockatiels are gregarious, but the greatest number of young are produced when pairs are separate but within sight and hearing range of other breeding pairs. A flighted (or unflighted) compartment

Opposite top: *The average cockatiel nest contains three to ten eggs.* **Opposite bottom:** *A three-day-old cockatiel and its day-old sibling. The egg tooth is located at the tip of the upper mandible.* **Above:** *At the age of 32 days, the young cockatiel is ready to leave the nest.* **Right:** *A young cockatiel, only a few hours after leaving its nest.*

should be at least 2½ feet in width to allow flying room for the birds.

A sleeping and feeding shelter and an outside wire flight are the necessary sections of an uncontrolled flighted aviary for cockatiels or for a mixed collection of birds. The sleeping quarters should be well constructed and free from dampness and drafts. Cockatiels may not require a heater during winter, but freezing temperature within the shelter must be avoided.

The wire flight itself can be covered with ordinary wire mesh or with the newer welded wire mesh. Cockatiels are large birds, and ¾ or one-inch mesh will be adequate, while a mixed collection will require ½ or ⅝ inch mesh. Heavy gauge wire with a coat of long-lasting non-toxic paint can also be used. This wire has a very long and useful life.

Many breeders have found that if a part of the top of the wired flight next to the sleeping quarters is covered with fiberglass or plastic sheeting, the birds can enjoy the flight during wet or snowy weather. The upper sides can also be covered with clear plastic for protection of both adult and young birds. The floor of the sleeping quarters should be secured against vermin. Concrete, heavy wooden boards, and precast stone slabs may be used to protect the sleeping quarter floor, while the floor of the wire flight may be either grassed over, covered with fine gravel or sand, or grass and gravel may be combined. Possible entry of rodents can be prevented by sinking an "L" shaped strip of ½ inch (small mesh) wire netting about eight inches into the ground, completely encircling the aviary. This procedure should keep out all rats and larger mice; smaller ones can be exterminated before they mature. Patented mouse baits found at pet shops and drug stores can efficiently destroy these rodents. Most, however, are detrimental to nesting birds and should not be used, as they foul the water and food and often cause health hazards.

The perches in the wire flights should be decorative, but, more importantly, they must give the birds the maximum amount of flying space. If the flight is grassed, then the portion beneath the

The cockatiel's cage should never be place near poisonous plants such as this poinsettia.

perches should be cleared and filled in with sand or gravel for easy cleaning. Any type of perch can be used in the sleeping quarters as long as all are firmly fixed. They should not be placed directly above seed, grit, or water holders. This precaution applies to all bird housings.

The seed vessels ought to be good, solid utensils that will stand firmly on a shelf, table or floor. They can be made of pottery, earthenware, glass or galvanized metal. These necessary vessels should be placed in an accessible spot for both the birds and the keeper.

Older garden sheds, stables, garages, conservatories and verandas may be converted into controlled breeding pens

Above: *Cockatiels that are reared by hand often remain tame after several years of aviary life.* **Left:** *Most cockatiels spend part of their day preening themselves.* **Opposite:** *Pied cockatiels often vary greatly in their plumage patterns. A symmetrical pattern is most desirable.*

by thorough cleaning, redecoration and installation of wire pens. The breeder's requirements will determine the size and number of pens. These pens ought to be about 6½ feet high by not less than three feet wide. The aviary should have a wire top to facilitate the catching of birds. Always bear in mind the dangers of limited space, which can adversely affect breeding.

Certain buildings may be converted into flighted aviaries by adding a flight onto one side. Breeders often like to demonstrate their creativity by making these adapted flights as attractive as possible. Flowering plants, hedges and other assorted evergreens can give the birds protection from the wind in addition to beautifying an outdoor aviary setting. Be sure, however, that no plants placed near the birds will be poisonous to them.

Cockatiels do reproduce in cages with a reasonable amount of freedom. The

A variety of cockatiel feeding vessels is available at your local pet shop.

Most cockatiels enjoy taking baths. You may wish to provide them with a commercially made bird bath, available at most local pet shops.

breeder does have complete control over his birds by using breeding cages. The birds should only be housed in such cages for the duration of the breeding period; at other times they should have the freedom of pens or flights. If the birds are kept in cages all the time, they tend to deteriorate in general quality and in breeding potential. The cages for a single breeding pair or for half a dozen birds should be approximately four feet long by two feet wide and three feet high.

Nest boxes can be hung on the side walls of cages to maximize internal space. The inspection of nests will be easier, and during non-breeding periods the side entrance holes can be covered with hinged flaps. If bird room space is extremely limited, nest boxes can be hung onto wire fronts, but whenever possible sides should be used, even if it means having one less tier of cages. The perches should be arranged as far apart as convenient, but with enough space so the tails of the birds and flight feathers do not rub against the sides. Nest boxes of the same type can be used for cages, pens, and aviaries.

The number of cockatiels kept as single family household pets has grown considerably in the past few years as people discover their charm. These birds are quite content living in the usual round or square all-wire parrot cages or in wire-fronted cages. Pet cockatiels should be taken into a household as soon as they can feed on their own, which is approximately seven to eight weeks after hatching. Like all birds, each cockatiel differs in temperament; some are naturally tame and friendly, while others require coaxing and patience. There are only a few birds that are not steady enough to tame. If after a reasonable amount of time the bird is found to be untrainable, some pet dealers may let the bird be returned to an aviary for a replacement. Do, however, find this out in advance.

The best time to obtain a bird for training is during the spring and summer months. At

When choosing a cockatiel from a large group, be sure to pick the healthiest specimen. In addition, if you believe that a sick bird is present in a particular cage, do not choose a bird from there, as illness spreads quickly among birds.

Most cockatiels enjoy taking baths. You may wish to provide them with a commercially made bird bath, available at most local pet shops.

this time the most suitable young birds are for sale. It is best to take a new bird home early in the day so it can have the maximum amount of time to settle down in its new quarters before nightfall. During the first few hours, the bird should be left quietly on its own so it can explore and adjust to its new cage without disturbance. The bird will usually settle down after a few days. The owner can then teach his pet to talk; its name is usually the easiest to learn, followed by short, simple, uncomplicated sentences. Once a bird is finger tamed it can be let loose in a room and taught to perform simple toy tricks. Generally, cock birds are the easiest to train as talking pets, but, naturally, a number of hens also fulfill the requirements. Cockatiels can be taught to talk by using the same methods that are used in training parrots and parakeets. The word or short phrase is repeated to it as often as possible.

Cockatiels are often recommended as pets because they are easy to feed and are not unreasonably expensive. They are perfect for both young people and adults.

Below: *The wire used for cockatiel cages and aviaries must be strong; it must also be small enough to prevent the cockatiel from squeezing through the bars and escaping.* **Opposite:** *A pair of normal gray cockatiels inside their cage.*

Feeding and Foods

Cockatiels thrive and breed well on a simply prepared diet of seeds. The main seed mixture consists of mixed millets, bulk canary seeds, oats, mixed sunflower seeds, some hemp, and panicum millet. Both young and old birds are partial to ears of small millet seeds known as millet sprays. Young birds that have just left their nests will learn to feed themselves more quickly if they eat millet sprays. These sprays are also helpful in training cockatiels for exhibition purposes. Some breeders soak the millet sprays in cold water for twenty-four hours at breeding times; this practice, however, can stimulate the growth of molds. The breeder has his choice of the soaked or dry varieties.

Cockatiels must be given a regular supply of various fresh green foods if they are to maintain a fit, healthy and vigorous condition throughout the year. These birds eat foods such as chickweed, seeding grasses, spinach, lettuce, cabbage hearts, brussel sprouts, sowthistles, watercress, shepherds purse, chicory, and slices of apples and carrots. All the green food should be given fresh daily and obtained from known clean sources. Sprouted seeds are also a good source of valuable food nutrients and are relished by parent birds when raising young. Seeds should be allowed to soak in water for 24 hours, and after this should just kept moist and in contact with air. When the tiny sprouts are visible, they are ready for feeding. One can also grow seedlings in a tray or pan. Small seeds are sprinkled in a pan with about one to two inches of moist clean soil and are allowed to sprout and develop into small seedlings. To conserve moisture, the pan can be covered with a plastic sheet. The whole tray or pan is then offered to the birds, who will devour the seedlings, leaves, roots and all. Uneaten food should be removed before it becomes stale or moldy.

Ample supplies of grit, cuttlefish bone, and mineral block are important to good health and perfect feathers.

Opposite: *Cockatiels kept in captivity must be given a nutritious, well-balanced diet that provides the nutrients found in the diet of wild birds.*

Additional mineral elements can be found in crushed dried domestic hen's eggshells, chalk, river and sea sand, and old mortar rubble.

Individual breeders have diverse ideas as to the best seed mixture for birds. There are, however, certain guidelines to follow. A mixture should not contain less than 40% of canary seed; added to this should be some 25% of mixed sunflower seeds coupled with a 35% mixture containing mixed millet, clipped oats, and a small quantity of hemp seed. Hemp, like sunflower seed, contains a high oil content and must be given in limited quantities which may be slightly increased during the cold winter months.

There are two major practices in giving seeds to cockatiels and other similar birds. One technique favors all the seeds being mixed together in one dish, while the other approves of giving canary, sunflower and the other mixed seeds in three separate dishes or "cafeteria" style. Both methods are appropriate. A problem can

A pair of pearled cockatiels enjoying a meal of mixed seeds and green food. Sufficient food must be provided for all cockatiels kept together.

Be certain that all foods given to your cockatiel are safe, especially green foods. In addition, do not allow your cockatiel access to your household plants.

arise if an odd bird gets hooked on a particular type of seed. This can make a bird too fat, which is certainly not desirable.

Soft food greatly helps cockatiels during breeding and molting periods. This food can take the form of a 50:50 mixture consisting of egg or nestling food (as used for canaries) and a good insectivorous food. If the birds do not like this ratio, the owner may juggle the proportions until a happy balance is found. Occasionally a variation may be used. Whole meal bread moistened with plain water, boiled milk, honey water, or glucose and water can be offered. All uneaten soft food should be removed from cages, pens, or aviaries at the end of each day to prevent the birds from eating stale or sour food. Single pet cockatiels also benefit from this type of food.

Most cockatiels like to take baths. Facilities are often provided for the bird's pleasure. Large, flat, shallow dishes, especially those made of earthenware, are best suited for this purpose and should be an addition to the bird's normal drinking vessel. If it is not possible to have a bathing dish in the pet cage, then a fine bird spray will do the job. When the bird becomes very tame it can bathe in the kitchen sink or in a bathroom under a slow dripping cold water tap.

Water used for drinking purposes can be placed in vessels similar to those used for seed feeding. Clip-on containers, which are better utilized in pens and cages, and water fountains, which are recommended for aviaries, also make good water vessels. These containers should all be

Seeds are the basic element in the cockatiel diet. Ask your veterinarian or pet shop dealer to help you create a healthy seed mixture for your bird.

Water vessels must be cleaned daily without fail. Cleanliness is essential in the life of a healthy cockatiel.

placed clear of perches and away from seed and grit pots.

Mixed grits ought to be given in flat dishes and separated from other mineral elements such as chalk, old mortar rubble, and crushed dried domestic hen's eggshells. These latter materials should be placed in separate dishes. Pieces of cuttlefish bone and mineral blocks should be firmly fixed so the birds can easily gnaw at them. If they are not attached they will be dropped, pulled about, and consequently soiled.

43

Breeding

Cockatiels are universally considered one of the most free-breeding members of the parrot family. Their breeding management is similar to that of the budgerigar. The quantity of cockatiels being produced has unquestionably led to the many color mutations that have further increased the bird's culture.

If strains are to be viable, only fully matured birds of the best quality can be bred. Most cockatiels will attempt to breed before they are 12 months old, but using immature birds can be a disaster at a later date. The best breeding results are achieved by breeding birds no younger than 18 to 24 months old. These mature birds can be expected to produce healthy young for four or five seasons.

Closely related birds should not be bred together; inbreeding of stock leads to the production of inferior young. Only very experienced breeders who have special knowledge of inbreeding and have a definite objective in view should be allowed to inbreed their birds. Indiscriminate breeding from closely related stock invariably leads to poor quality birds (some with abnormalities)

being produced, along with a sharp decline in the health, substance and breeding potential of the stud.

The initial stock of birds should be unrelated and procured from widely separate breeding studs. If these birds are not ringed with either closed or split rings, the new owner should ring them on receipt of the birds. Metal and celluloid split rings can also be used for this purpose. Closed metal rings are permanent; they identify the birds and allow the breeder to make and keep positive breeding records. They are also available with etched coded numbers. When stock birds are first received, their ring number or ring color should be entered in a register along with any other particulars. Within several seasons the owner will have a complete history of the stock inscribed in the register. This method will enable the breeder to mate the stock

Opposite: *Cockatiels are free breeders in captivity as well as in the wild.*

without any problems caused by close inbreeding or by split character mistakes that are carried by the birds.

A positive and permanent identification can be made of the young cockatiels by having them ringed with numbered and year-dated closed metal rings when they are between six and ten days old. The chick being ringed is held in the hand with one leg between the thumb and the first finger. The three longest toes are brought together as the ring is slipped along the shank and over the small hind toe. The small toe is then pulled free of the ring with the aid of a toothpick, matchstick or similar object. The chick may squeak quite loudly during this procedure, but it is not from being hurt—it is due to its indignity at being handled. Nests of chicks can

Cuttlebone should be provided for the cockatiel at all times, but it is especially important if you plan to breed your bird.

A pair of normal gray cockatiels examining a nest box. The breeding pair may spend some time getting acquainted with their new accommodations before actually breeding.

be identified on sight by attaching colored celluloid rings with the closed rings. These colored rings allow the breeder to single out specific birds in the flights without having to catch and handle them.

The majority of healthy, fully mature cockatiels are ready to begin breeding in the spring around the beginning of March. The weather is becoming amenable, the days are growing longer and warmer, and a supply of numerous fresh green foods is becoming easier to obtain. Many breeders prefer to leave their mated pairs together all the time, while other owners opt to split up the pairs at the end of each breeding season. When the pairs are separated, the sexes are kept apart in flights until they are needed for the next breeding season. This is the practice followed by most budgerigar breeders. Both these methods work well depending upon the available accommodations. It is up to the breeder to decide what he thinks will be most practical and effective for his stock.

Many experts favor the pairs being split apart, with the sexes being kept in separate

Cockatiels need a period of acquaintance before settling down to raise a brood. Mutual preening often takes place at this time.

Before placing a true pair of cockatiels together for breeding, be sure that the birds are genetically compatible for the result you have in mind.

accommodations, to achieve the best results from color breeding. This method not only allows the breeder to maintain strict control over the birds, but it also prevents the possibility of unwanted crossbreeding. In addition, an advanced breeder may want to conduct experimental pairing with his stock; it is very important that there be no doubt with respect to the parentage of the bird used.

Prior to the actual breeding season, prospective pairings should be made on paper, with each bird's pedigree checked against the stock register. This technique will ensure that the breeder chooses the right crosses to give the most satisfactory results and that closely related birds are not mated together. The pedigrees of all breeding pairs used in color matching must be checked annually. This procedure is very important and includes all normals or mutations.

If mated pairs have been left together in aviaries, pens or cages during the year, the breeder can position nest boxes when he feels his birds are fully fit and ready for breeding. Pairs that are freshly mated should be given five to seven days to become properly acquainted before giving them nest boxes. In this time they can settle down, mate, and get in the right mood for succesful reproduction.

A pair of pearled cockatiels enjoying sunflower seeds. Pearled cockatiels with a great deal of white in their wings are sometimes called lacewings.

A beautiful white male cockatiel. A good white cockatiel specimen is considered quite a prize in the bird fancy.

It is usual for clutches of eggs to start appearing in the nest boxes 15 to 20 days after fully fit, ready-to-breed adult matched pairs are brought together. The number of eggs per clutch can range from three to ten; most of the large clutches are produced by older mature hens. The eggs are glossy white, oval in shape, and vary from 26 to 28 mm by 19 to 21 mm in size. Cockatiels, like budgerigars, lay their eggs on alternate days. This means there will be a few days' difference between the hatching of the first and last chicks of a nest. Actually, the length of time is governed by whether or not the parents start to sit from the first or subsequent eggs. Each egg has an incubation period of 21 days. The parents will take equal care of the young regardless of their age. It is extremely rare for the smallest chicks in a nest come to any harm.

Whether an egg is fertile or not is easily tested by candling. A fertile egg, when seen through a strong source

A pair of cockatiels mating. Both parent birds will usually take part in feeding the chicks.

Cockatiel parents will care for all chicks. It is rare for a baby bird to be neglected.

of light (lighted candle, flashlight, sunlight), shows traces of the developing embryo surrounded by a network of blood capillaries. Infertile eggs are clear; they should be removed from the nest.

Newly hatched cockatiel chicks, covered with long, yellowish, silky down, are usually considered ugly; it is not until other feathers develop that they begin to look like birds. Both members of breeding pairs will take their turn at incubating the eggs. Cock birds sit during the day, while their partners sit at night. Both sexes equally share the duty of feeding the young, but cock birds do not seem to feed their mates while young are in the nest. Males appear to think that feeding the hens is a waste of time, since the female then passes the food on to the chicks, so they may just as well feed the young directly. Cockatiels usually do not mind if a breeder inspects the nest boxes, as long as this is not done too frequently. It is rare to find a pair deserting their young as a protest against the nest interference.

There are numerous varieties of nest boxes that can be used for cockatiels. The most popular among breeders are the upright and flat types. The upright nest box is approximately 15 inches deep, ten inches wide and long, with a 2½ inch square or round entrance hole near the top. Just below this entrance, a perch is fixed and a hinged door is on the top for easy inspection. The dimensions of the flat type are ten inches deep by ten inches wide by 15

Be sure to provide enough nest boxes for all couples that will be bred. In addition, separate any single birds from the breeding area, as they may cause trouble.

The nest box should provide a perch in the front. This allows the parents to stop before entering the nest, which will prevent a fast entry that can damage the eggs or hurt the chicks.

inches long with the entrance hole and perch at one side and the inspection door on the top. These measurements can be somewhat varied if it suits the breeder's particular requirements. It is convenient to have loose, concave bottoms covered with either a good layer of peat, coarse pine saw dust, soft wood shavings (or chips), or a mixture of these materials. These materials help prevent the eggs from rolling. The majority of nesting hen birds seem to prefer a mixture of materials.

Young cockatiels are fully feathered and ready to leave their nest boxes when they are approximately five weeks old. Due to differences in hatching times, several days will elapse before an entire nest has flown. The young birds are fed by their parents for a week or ten days after they have left the nest. The owner should not move the birds from the breeding quarters until he is certain that the young can adequately fend for themselves. The chicks must have access to plenty of the usual seed, millet sprays, grits and various fresh green food both before and after they are taken from their parents.

When necessary, some breeders favor the practice of fostering eggs and chicks. Some eggs may have been abandoned; if fertile, they are transferred to other nests with eggs of about the same age. This is the one instance when having more than one pair of birds mate at about the same time is desirable. However, be sure that the eggs are

Breeding cockatiels must be provided with an enriched diet. This diet should be somewhat higher in oil content than their usual diet.

Before any cockatiels are selected to be bred, the owner must be certain that the birds are in excellent condition.

identified and the ensuing chicks banded as early as possible.

Parents may stop feeding or start feather picking one or more chicks. In this situation, the alternatives are either to hand-feed or foster these young. Hand-feeding is possible, but it is tedious, time-consuming and impractical when one has many birds to care for. In fostering, the chick is placed in a nest with chicks of about the same age; foster parents may refuse a much younger chick and it may be left to perish.

Cockatiel Color Varieties

In these sections, color descriptions will be given of the major types of cocks and hens. These detailed descriptions of areas of color will enable readers to visualize the birds more clearly as they look at the illustrations that appear within this book. Although there were no actual subspecies recorded among the wild flocks, there are, however, some slight tone differences in birds taken from widely separated habitats. These slight differences can also be seen in various domesticated strains along with their mutant colors.

NORMAL GRAY COCKATIEL

Domesticated cockatiels derived from wild-type birds are more substantially built than the newer mutant colors and, for this reason, are used extensively for outcrossing. There are many first-class strains of pure normals from which exhibition birds are derived. Overall substance and general depth of color can be improved by carefully selecting parent birds—in fact, this is the only way a color strain may be developed with the quality being maintained.

Most household pet cockatiels are of the normal gray type. All colors are equal in their talking and taming potential; however, birds of new color mutations are more expensive.

Pairs of normal grays will produce only gray offspring, except in cases of chance mutation or of a gene which, unknown to the breeder, carries a mutant color. If a lot of crossbreeding takes place for the sake of stock improvement, then second and third generation birds will often be disposed of as normals.

Cock: The general overall color of the body comprises various shades of gray: the deepest tone is on the underside of the long pointed tail, and the palest shade of gray is found along the two center feathers. The front of the head, cheeks and throat are lemon yellow, and the outward curving crest

Opposite: *A pair of normal gray cockatiels. Note the orange patches on the cheeks.*

(approximately 1-1¼ inches long) is a mixture of yellow and gray. The sides of the head are white with large red-orange patches. There is a broad white bar on each wing tinted very pale yellow; this bar runs from the shoulders to the secondary wing coverts. Each wing has a broad white bar tinted with very light yellow extending from the "elbow" across the wing coverts. The eyes are brown, while the beak, feet, and legs are gray of various intensities. Total length including the tail is approximately 13 inches.

Hen: The general body color is very much like the cock's except that the wing bars and eye patches are less pure in color. The ear patches are not as extensive in the female, and the crown lacks white. The yellow areas are only very

Headstudy of a normal gray cockatiel. The normal gray variety is often called the wild color.

The normal gray cock is usually slightly larger than the female. In addition, the plumage of the male has purer color than that of the female.

faintly tinted. In fact, the yellow areas tend to be more grayish in hue. The hen's thighs are barred with pale yellow and the underside of her tail is striped and dappled with gray and yellow; the overall gray coloring is duller than on the cock and often has a faint brownish cast on it. A very mature hen's general color deepens quite considerably and it becomes difficult to distinguish them from first-year cocks. Hens are about 11-12 inches in total length.

Immature birds: These are paler editions of the hen. They do not get yellow on their facial area until they are approximately six months old, and it is not until several months later that they assume full adult coloring. Feathered cockatiel nestlings are difficult to sex. Those with the brightest colors usually turn out to be cocks, but this color test is not always true; do not take it as a sure guide.

LUTINO COCKATIEL

The color differences between this mutation and the normal gray quickly caught the imagination of many breeders of parrotlike birds. Lutino cockatiels are white ground birds like the gray or blue series in budgerigars, and therefore possess red-orange ear patches and varying amounts of yellow suffusion on their bodies. Genetically, the lutino character removes all dark coloring from a bird's plumage, but does not affect the yellow or red-orange color; these light and dark hues are produced by entirely different pigments. This fact causes many breeders to call these birds yellows, especially those lutinos with an extra amount of yellow suffusion. Yellowness may be increased in depth and extent by careful selection of the breeding stock.

Cock: Pure white is found in the general areas that are gray in the normal cockatiel. The

Left: *A lutino cockatiel. This particular bird has red eyes and would be called an albino by some fanciers.* **Opposite:** *Note how the lutino cockatiel maintains the yellow and orange coloration on its head.*

Note the pinkish legs on this lutino cockatiel.

throat, part of the cheeks, and front of the head are lemon yellow. The crest is a mixture of yellow and white, and the ear patches are the normal shade of red-orange. The wings have areas of yellow. There is a yellow cast or tinge on the tail. The eyes are red, the beak is a yellow horn color, and the feet and legs are flesh pink.

Hen: A yellow cast on the thighs and under the tail differentiates the general coloring between the two sexes.

Immature birds: These young show less yellowing than adults and are difficult to sex until they are fully matured. Their eyes are a lighter but brighter shade of red than those of an adult.

Even some fully adult lutinos are difficult to sex, and only by careful observation of their behavior towards one another can they be sexed.

Genetics: The character that causes lutino coloring is sex-linked in the manner of inheritance. By making certain pairings, the breeder can use sex-linked mutations to control the sex of a color. This knowledge can be very useful when young cock birds are needed to train as tame talking pets. The rules of lutino inheritance will show the breeder what matings can be made so young cocks can be identifiable at hatching.

1) Lutino cock x lutino hen gives 100% lutino cocks and

A trio of lutino cockatiels. Young lutinos are usually less yellow than adults, and they are often difficult to sex.

hens. 2) Lutino cock x normal gray hen gives 50% normal gray/lutino cocks, 50% lutino hens. 3) Lutino hen x normal gray cock gives 50% normal gray/lutino cocks, 50% normal gray hens. 4) Lutino hen x normal gray/lutino cock gives 25% lutino cocks, 25% lutino hens, 25% normal gray/lutino cocks, 25% normal gray hens. 5) Normal gray/lutino cock x normal gray hen gives 25% normal gray cocks, 25% normal gray hens, 25% normal gray/lutino cocks, 25% lutino hens.

Presently, the majority of lutinos in existence are the lutino form of the normal gray. It is possible, however, to have a lutino form of all the other mutations both in their pure and "split" form, all of which look alike. Because of this, lutino parents carrying various color characters may have young of different colors in their nests. The breeder will be able to discover the reason why other colors have appeared if he keeps good and accurate records. An undesirable character,

Breeders enjoy the challenge of working with the cockatiel color varieties and with improving the type of the birds.

A lovely, evenly marked pied cockatiel. The pied cockatiel is sometimes called the harlequin.

baldness, has appeared in lutino cockatiels, and breeders are trying very hard to eliminate this apparently dominant trait from their stock.

PIED COCKATIEL

Breeders have tried for many years to produce the pied (also known as variegated) cockatiel. Birds were being bred with extra odd white feathers in their plumage, but these mismarked specimens were not pied cockatiels. It was not until a mutation appeared that the pied strain was finally established. The

67

character that gives the broken color appearance is recessive and can be carried by other colors, both by cock and hen, in "split" form.

Cock: These birds are similar in color to the normal gray and have patches of different sizes that interrupt the dark color. These clear, irregularly shaped patches are white and yellow tinted with white. Individual birds have assorted clear areas; some specimens possess small patches, while others are extensively marked. Most of the birds seem to have a 50:50

Pied cockatiels are difficult birds to perfect, as the symmetry of their markings is subject to great variation.

A normal/pied cockatiel. This bird was produced by the breeding of a normal gray cockatiel with a pied.

color arrangement. The beak and eyes are like those of a normal gray, but the feet and legs can be gray, fleshy pink, or a mixture of both.

Hen: The female is similar to the normal gray and like the cock has white and yellow tinted with white areas that break the basic color of the plumage.

Immature birds: The young are merely paler versions of the hen. They do not have clearly defined lines of demarcation in their broken areas.

Genetics: When a pied normal gray cock or hen is paired to a normal gray, all the young produced will be normal gray in color, but genetically they will be different. Birds resulting from the crossing of these two colors are known as normal gray/pied, and when given suitable mates they can produce actual pied young. The pied character is inherited in the usual recessive manner.

1) Pied normal gray x normal gray gives 100% normal gray/pied cocks and hens. 2) Pied normal gray x normal gray pied gives 50% pied normal gray cocks and hens. 3) Normal gray/pied x normal gray/pied gives 25% normal gray cocks and hens, 50% normal gray/pied cocks and hens, 25% pied normal gray cocks and hens. 4) Normal gray/pied x normal gray gives 50% normal gray cocks and hens, 50% normal gray/pied cocks and hens. 5) Pied

When breeding cockatiels, it is a good idea to remember that, just like people, all birds are individuals.

It is possible to produce a white cockatiel by selectively breeding pied birds.

normal gray x pied normal gray gives 100% pied normal gray cocks and hens.

Since there is no sex-linkage involved, it is immaterial as to which member of a pair is the pied normal gray or the "split."

Notice that in crossings 3) and 4), two genetic types are produced which have no visual difference; this can only be discovered by test pairing.

It is essential that normal gray/pieds be used regularly in

Headstudy of a pearled cockatiel. Pearled cockatiels have a change of feather pattern, not a change of color.

pairings if a stud of the pied normal gray is to be improved and maintained. The best results are obtained when the "split" birds are from crossing normal gray to pied normal gray. This rule applies to all color matings where "split" birds are used. The birds from such crosses are known as first cross "splits."

Bear in mind that it is possible to produce actual clear white (but non-albino) birds by selective breeding. Cockatiels with the largest clear areas can be bred together to produce young with a greater expanse of light feathers. After generations of this selective pairing, it is possible that the desired objective of clear white birds may be reached. Such whites have dark eyes.

PEARLED COCKATIEL

The pearled mutation is an unexpected happening. Like the opaline in the budgerigar family, the originally named pearled has a change of feather pattern—not a change of color.

Pearled cockatiels are fairly recent arrivals, so they are relatively limited in number and

A young, finger tame pearled cockatiel. Pearled cockatiels are still relatively uncommon.

tend to be somewhat expensive. Several birds have appeared at exhibitions where they have been greatly admired, and more than ever, there is an increasing demand for this novel variety.

This bird's inheritance is sex-linked like the lutino. The expectations for pearled mating can be worked out by adapting those obtained for lutino matings. There can be pearled forms of other mutations; so far, pied pearled and fawn pearled have been produced by enthusiastic breeders.

Breeders have found that the pearled character of the plumage persists in the females but fades in the males after the first molt or later in the second year. Therefore, banding of the birds is quite important, for the character may not be recognized visually.

Cock: These birds are somewhat like the normal gray, but vary in wing pattern. Two shades of gray coloring occupy large areas of wing feathers which create a definite, attractive pattern combination. The pattern on the wings is variable in its markings and in the sex-linked nature of its inheritance. The orange-red color of the ear patches and the yellow suffusion on certain areas are not as intense as on the normal gray. The eyes are clear brown and the beak is gray. The feet and legs are in different tones of gray; sometimes they even have a pinkish undertone.

Hen: The female's general body color is like the cock, but there are a few exceptions. Her ear patches are not as extensive, nor are they as rich as the male's, and her wing bars are less pure in color. The white on the crown is absent, and the yellow areas are a bit fainter than they are on the cock. Her thighs are barred with pale yellow and the underside of the tail is striped and dappled with clear gray and yellow.

Immature birds: These young are paler than the adults. Their pattern markings are less clear and more variable in their distribution.

Opposite: *A cinnamon cock and a lutino hen. In order to keep producing quality birds of various color varieties, breeders must exercise strict control over the matings between individual birds.*

Rare Cockatiel Color Varieties

Cockatiel breeding has greatly increased in recent years, and soon there should be additional color varieties developed. As each new mutation appears, the number of possible composite types increase, and excitement is added to the already challenging world of breeding and exhibiting of cockatiels.

FAWN (CINNAMON) COCKATIEL

With the domestication of most species of birds, sooner or later there will appear a cinnamon form in yellow ground birds and a fawn form in white ground birds. Fawns (cinnamon) were reported to have been bred a considerable time ago, but it was not until recently that details and live specimens became available. It was not recorded when these mutations first appeared, but examples have turned up in Australia, America and Europe during the last 25 years. In Europe, this mutation is called cinnamon or Isabelle. These birds ought to be termed "fawn," for they are white ground birds just like canaries and zebra finches where a white ground bird is involved. The actual color of fawn cockatiels is more of a gray-brown than the cinnamon-brown shade commonly associated with other domestic birds.

All fawn (cinnamon) varieties have pinkish, flesh color eyes when they are first hatched. This characteristic sharply contrasts with the similar black-eyed normal grays. This trait does, however, enable a breeder to immediately identify fawns that were produced by crossbreedings while they are still in the nest.

Fawn cockatiels do offer plenty of scope for color improvement, as their general overall color may be developed into a brown shade. This can be done by selecting the best colored fawns and mating them with pale normals, and then by mating the resulting birds together. After a few seasons of careful selection, the color of fawns should be improved. The objective is to eliminate all gray overtones.

Opposite: *Cockatiels continue to produce new color varieties. These new colors have added much interest to the cockatiel fancy.*

Cocks: The general overall body color is a variety of grayish brown hues. The deepest tone is on the underside of the long pointed tail, while the palest shade is found within the two central feathers. The front of the head, cheeks and throat are lemon yellow, and the crest is a mixture of yellow and grayish brown. The sides of the crown are white. The large ear patches are red-orange. Each wing has a broad white bar tinted pale yellow that runs

A trio of lutino cockatiels. The lutino mutation is, so far, the only one which does not visibly combine with others.

Several new cockatiels have been created through the use of the pearled cockatiel in breeding programs.

from the elbow to the secondary wing coverts. The eyes are brown, the beak is grayish horn in color, and the feet and legs are pinkish.

Hens: The female is very much like the male in general body color, except that her ear patches are not as extensive nor as rich in color. The wing bars are also less pure in color. The white is absent from the crown and the yellow areas are only faintly tinted and tend to be more grayish brown. The thighs are barred with yellow, while the underside of the tail is striped and spotted with grayish brown and yellow. Like the normal gray, the color deepens with age in very mature hens, and it becomes difficult to distinguish them from the first year cocks.

Immature birds: These young are paler editions of the hen. They do not get yellow on their facial areas until they are several months old, and it is not until they are in their eighth to tenth month that they assume full adult coloring.

THE DILUTE COCKATIEL
Most breeds of domesticated birds will eventually produce a dilute mutation where the color is seen in varying degrees less than its full strength. These birds are paler and brighter than normal grays and are

A silver cockatiel. The silver cockatiel is the result of a dilute mutation in the normal gray cockatiel.

The silver cockatiel is a recent mutation. It is believed that this trait is inherited recessively.

often called dilute or silver cockatiels. Since this mutation is relatively new, information about these birds is somewhat scant. The dilute mutation is now considered a recessive breeding type by most breeders. It is possible that these birds have been developed by selective pairings of pale normal grays over a period of time. Dilute birds are really paler and brighter gray than the normal gray and deserve to be called silver. If this coloration is indeed man-made, then it demonstrates what can be done with perseverance and care in breeding aviaries. As sufficient stock becomes available, more breeding experiments will be engaged, and soon their status will be completely answered.

Since the dilute form is recessive, it will be inherited in the same manner as the pied character.

Cock: The dilute has the characteristic lemon yellow on its cheeks, throat, and front of head. Its general overall body color consists of shades of silver-gray. Again, the deepest tones are found along the underside of the long pointed tail, and the palest color is located within the two central feathers. The large ear

A pair of adult cinnamons in an outdoor aviary. The cinnamon cockatiel is often called the Isabelle.

A silver male cockatiel. As in most cockatiel color varieties, the male birds are more brightly colored than the females.

patches are red-orange, and the sides of the crown are white. The dilute has reddish-brown eyes, a grayish beak, and pinkish legs and feet. Each wing has a broad white bar with pale yellow running its course from the elbow to the secondary wing coverts.

Hen: Its general body color is similar to the cock, but the ear patches are not as large or as bright. The wing bars are less pure in color, the underside of the tail is striped and dappled with yellow and silver-gray, and the thighs are barred with yellow. The hen lacks white on her crown and has faintly tinted yellow areas that are actually more silver-gray than the cock.

Immature birds: Like other cockatiels, these are the paler edition of the hen.

COMPOSITE COLOR VARIETIES

It is possible through a series of matings to produce a cockatiel that shows the characters of two or more mutations. The only existing mutation that does not visually combine with others is the lutino, and this is due to its overall loss of dark coloring. The pied can be bred in fawn (fawn here is always understood to be connected with cinnamon), pearled, and dilute forms. It is also possible to have pied fawn pearled, pied fawn dilute, and pied pearled dilute cockatiels. The pearled can be had in pearled fawn, pearled dilute, and pearled fawn dilute.

It takes at least two seasons to produce a combination of

A pair of pearled pied cockatiels in an outdoor aviary.

A pearled pied cockatiel. It takes at least two breeding seasons to produce the pied character—it may, however, take much longer than that.

the pied character since it is recessive. After this amount of time, production is relatively simple. The pied pearled can be bred by crossing a pearled cock with a normal pied gray hen. This cross produces normal gray/pearled cocks and normal gray/pied hens. The next season, normal gray/pied cocks can be paired to normal gray pied hens, and this will give 25% pied pearled gray hens among the young. This procedure will give the breeder the correct stock for the following season if he wishes to produce both cocks and hens of the pied pearled gray form.

The pied fawn can be bred similarly to the pied pearled, since the fawn character is also sex-linked. The first step in this project involves pairing a fawn cock to a pied hen. This cross gives normal gray/pied fawn cocks and normal gray/pied hens. When these young cocks are paired back to normal pied hens, they give 25% of the desired pied fawn hens. In the following year, cocks of this color can be bred by pairing the pied fawn hens to the "split" cocks.

Birds that have three color characters (pied, fawn and pearled) can be raised from a number of different crosses

Left: *Genetics is not an exact science, as the factors involved can get complicated. Remember that cockatiel breeding will always involve some risk.* **Opposite:** *A lovely pied cockatiel.*

where the birds have the necessary characters either visually or in "split" form. Once pied fawn cocks have been bred they can then be mated to pied pearled hens, which will produce normal pied/fawn pearled cocks and pied fawn hens. In turn, the normal pied/fawn pearled cocks can be mated to either pied pearled or pied fawn hens. From either of these matings will come some pied pearled fawn hens together with a number of other useful breeding birds.

The dilute (silver) character can be used to create further color varieties such as dilute (silver) pearled, dilute (fawn) dilute (silver) pied, dilute (silver) pearled fawn, dilute (silver) pied fawn, dilute (silver) pied pearled, and dilute (silver) pied pearled fawn. By including the dilute (silver) character in composite forms, the resulting birds are a softer shade of color which makes them distinct from the ordinary gray shade. A paler and somewhat altered tone of color is produced when the fawn character is introduced. Due to the basic color of cockatiels, the present mutant colors will be a little paler but will still be discernible from the normal gray. Since the number of mutations has been increasing, there can and will be a considerable number of different colors and combinations of the cockatiel.

A pearled pied cockatiel. This variety is becoming more and more popular among cockatiel fanciers.

Exhibiting Cockatiels

The potential of cockatiels as exhibition birds is just now being explored. Until recently, very few show-promoting societies had an actual separate class solely for cockatiels. At most shows, cockatiels must be exhibited in mixed parakeet classes with new colors going into abnormally colored classes. Many breeders would probably exhibit more of their birds if they were given encouragement in the form of separate classes. Breeders can help this situation by voicing their requests when local shows are considering classifications.

Cockatiels are excellent show birds, either as single or true pairs. They settle down quickly and become tame and

Left: *Cockatiels make good pets for mature, responsible children.* **Opposite:** *Most cockatiels become tame rather quickly; therefore, their temperament is suitable for exhibition.*

amenable in a show cage. At present there are no standard show cages required for cockatiels, and consequently they are exhibited in various types of cages deemed suitable by their owners. Many of these cages have a lengthwise perch that enables the birds to sit with their breast or back to the judge. Other breeders prefer to follow the style of the standard budgerigar show cage.

The budgerigar style show cage is excellent for the all-around appraisal of the bird's merits from an exhibition angle. A recommended size cage for a pair of cockatiels is 18 inches long by nine inches deep by 16 inches high, with two centrally placed perches. Until a standard show cage is adopted, cockatiels can be shown in any suitably sized

A lutino cockatiel in flight. Do not allow your cockatiel liberty unless it is properly supervised.

Before placing a show pair together in the same cage, allow the birds to become accustomed to each other.

cage. The cage should be clean and well painted with non-toxic paint.

To do well in a show, a cockatiel must have a reasonable amount of show training beforehand. When selecting birds for show, the relationship of the chosen birds is not important since this is not for breeding purposes.

The selected pairs should each be put into a stock cage (that is larger than four feet) weeks before they are required for actual showing. An old show cage can be hung over the open door of the stock cage with green food or millet sprays in it to entice the birds inside. After a short time the birds will be accustomed to

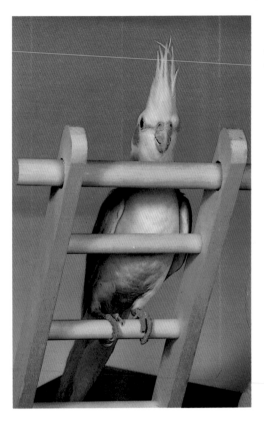

Whether you train your cockatiel for show or for pleasure, be sure to be patient and level-headed during the training sessions

going in and out of the show cage. Then they can be shut in for short periods at the beginning, and gradually the time of confinement can be increased. It is surprising how quickly these pairs adapt to the change in accommodation, for they soon become quite at ease in their smaller cages. In addition, a show cockatiel must be trained not to be afraid of strangers looking at it from close range. The judge cannot really evaluate a bird that is constantly moving or that is huddled in a corner of the cage. While the pairs are in the stock cages, a regular spraying with a fine water spray is helpful for keeping their plumage in the clean, silky condition required for exhibition.

Whether the show pairs are normal grays or a new color, the principle of selection is the same in all cases. Each bird should be a good, well-colored example of its variety and have plenty of substance, unbroken and clean feathers, a clean beak, and no toes or nails missing.

Normal birds are judged according to uniformity and quality of the gray coloration. Ticking (random white feathers among the gray) is considered a flaw. With specimens of the pied variety, the clear areas should match each other as nearly as possible; symmetry of piedness is a great

Each bird that is shown must have perfectly clean feathers which are in good condition.

consideration. Forty to 60% pied condition is adequate. It is also desirable to have more tail and flight feathers clear. With respect to the lutino cockatiel, some breeders prefer to develop either a more white bird or a more yellow bird. The bald spot is undesirable in the white variety of cockatiel for showing; no splotching is allowed.

Only true pairs of the same color can be shown together, so it is important to make well-balanced pairs. It is not advisable to exhibit any pair too frequently, especially if they are to be used later for breeding purposes.

Left: *The show bird must, of course, be fed a high quality, well-balanced diet.* **Opposite:** *A pair of lutino cockatiels. Some bird societies require that cockatiels be shown in pairs, while others allow single entries.*

Left: *Indoors or outdoors, the cockatiel is a lovely bird.* Below: *Seed and water vessels should be made of a non-porous, easy-to-clean material.* Opposite: *The proud, erect carriage and the magnificent crest are only two of the cockatiel's appealing characteristics.*

The Cockatiel as a Household Pet

Each year more and more people are keeping cockatiels as household pets. These birds are easy to tame and finger train and are reasonable in cost when compared to other members of the parrot family. The cockatiel is not a prolific talker, but it can be taught to repeat a number of words and short sentences.

Occasionally there will be a brilliant linguist among these birds.

To train as a tame talking pet, a young, fit, healthy cock bird should be selected and taken away from its parents as soon as it is seen feeding entirely on its own. Young hens can also be trained to become tame, talking,

Left: *The cockatiel's popularity continues to increase as more people come to appreciate its personality and beauty.* **Opposite:** *A lovely lutino cockatiel.*

Opposite: Judging by its color pattern alone, this pearled cockatiel could be either a female or an immature bird, but it could not be an adult male.
Right: *A pair of lutino cockatiels.*
Below: *This temporary cage is too small to use as permanent quarters for a pet cockatiel.*

affectionate pets, but they are more temperamental and take longer to learn to talk than the cock. The prospective owner may have to rely on the breeder or pet shop for correct information on sexing the bird.

A cage should be obtained for the bird before it is even purchased. The cage can be a box type sized to fit in with the furnishings of a room, or it can be a more conventional round or square metal wire parrot-type cage. Ample food, water, and grit vessels must be positioned in the cage together with a piece of cuttlefish bone

A variety of cage toys can be found at your local pet shop. Be sure, however, not to crowd the cage with too many toys.

The use of food rewards will help a great deal in training the cockatiel.

and a mineral nibble. The cage floor should be covered with sand or very fine gravel. The cage must be cleaned regularly.

It is best to get a bird early in the day so it has plenty of time to settle down in its new home well before roosting time. The bird should be allowed approximately eight to 12 days to become fully accustomed to its new surroundings before serious training is started. Some cockatiel owners, however, are of the opinion that a period of acclimation is not necessary and that young cockatiels can be tamed in a few hours.

Sudden movements and loud noises must not be made around the cage. If the bird is to be kept in a room used often

The normal gray cockatiel is still, despite the introduction of new color varieties, the most popular and inexpensive type of cockatiel. Shown here is a young male normal gray coming into color. Opposite: A fully adult male normal gray.

by the family, a cover should then be placed over the cage so the bird will not be frightened by noise. The owner should speak to the new bird in a quiet, clear, even voice when giving fresh seed and water to the bird. Only one person in the household ought to train the cockatiel at first; this is done to prevent the bird from being confused by different voice tones and inflections.

When an owner feels that his bird has become thoroughly accustomed to its new home, he can begin the first stages of training. The door should be

Below: *If you plan to house two or more cockatiels together, be sure the living space is adequate for the number of birds being kept there.* **Opposite:** *A lutino cockatiel that has been trained to perch on a bird stand.*

Left: *The eyes of a healthy pet cockatiel should be clear and bright at all times.* Below: *Most cockatiels love sunflower seeds. As sunflower seeds are fattening, however, they should not be given too often.*

opened and a piece of millet spray or green food should be offered slowly to the bird. Remember to hold the food steady as the bird nibbles at the offering. In most cases it does not take long before the bird is eating out of the owner's hands without showing signs of nervousness. The next step is to gradually ease a finger beneath the bird's feet so it can sit there while eating food from the other hand. As soon as the bird is sitting fearlessly, it can be pulled slowly towards the open door, out into the room, and then back into the cage.

Once a bird reaches such a stage of tameness, it will usually let the owner gently stroke its chest and tickle the back of its head.

After a while, the cage door can be left open to let the bird fly around the room and get some much needed exercise.

Be sure, however, to supervise your cockatiel whenever it is at liberty. Whenever the bird is out of its cage all doors and windows must be firmly closed and no solid fuel, gas or electric appliances should be in use. Cut flowers and potted plants ought to be removed

from the room since they attract cockatiels. If certain green plants are eaten, they will have a bad effect upon the bird's digestion.

A pet cockatiel can be easily fed with a mixture of sunflower seed, canary seed, mixed millets, and a few clipped oats. Sometimes new owners like to ask the breeder or pet store owner what kind of seed mixture the bird has been eating and what type should be used. Most cockatiels are extremely fond of various green foods, and whenever possible a small quantity should be given to them daily.

Care and consideration in housing, feeding and general overall management of a cockatiel is important if the pet is to give its owner years of

Left: *Millet sprays are probably the best food to use when training your pet cockatiel.* **Opposite:** *A normal gray male cockatiel.*

Opposite: *Cuttlebone, either in powdered or solid form, should always be available for your cockatiels. Cuttlebone is an excellent source of calcium for your birds.* **Above:** *A pair of lutino cockatiels.*

interesting and pleasurable companionship. There should not be any trouble healthwise if the bird was healthy when first obtained. If the bird does appear to be off color, or if it has very ruffled feathers or loose droppings, do seek advice. Bird breeders can often be of help, but in most cases the pet owner should seek veterinary assistance.

WING CLIPPING

An unclipped pet bird should never be taken outdoors

It is important for you to become acquainted with your cockatiel and its habits. If you are aware of your bird's normal, healthy behavior, you can spot when the bird is ill more quickly.

Some tame cockatiels would rather eat seed from their owners' hands than from their seed vessels.

uncaged; the chance of its flying away is great and the possibility of retrieving an escaped bird is often miniscule. If recapturing a bird is possible, some injury may result from the process. To ensure the safety of the bird, several means have been devised to prevent its flying away other than actual confinement in a cage. Even in the confines of a closed room, unclipped birds can injure themselves by flying straight into the wall or window pane. Birds kept in aviaries and flighted brooding pens do not need to be clipped, since they are fairly secure unless the keeper and his help are very careless and leave doors open.

Above left: *In the normal gray/pied mutation, it is preferable that most tail and wing feathers be clear, with the ideal being completely clear flight feathers. Symmetry of markings is more important than the degree of piedness.* **Above right:** *A lutino cockatiel.* **Opposite:** *A pair of adult cinnamon cockatiels. Cinnamons have eyes that are lighter brown than those of the normal grays.*

Wing clipping is a simple and painless procedure. It will not cause pain or harm unless the skin or flesh is damaged. With the aid of another person who holds the bird around the body firmly and spreads the wing out, one person cuts some particular feathers off one or both wings. There are two suggested styles of clipping: in one method all the primaries (principal flight feathers) are cut from either the left or right wing; in the other method some secondaries and the primaries (except a few outer ones) of both wings are cut. In the second method the symmetrical appearance of the wings is preserved. Wing clipping should never be done by an amateur; an experienced professional should be consulted for this procedure.

Instead of cutting the wing

Below: *Do not clip the wings of the cockatiel yourself unless you are quite experienced. Have your veterinarian or pet shop dealer do it for you.* **Opposite:** *Wing clipping should be done just prior to the cockatiel's first taming session.*

Opposite: *Lutino cockatiels are beautiful birds, but they are prone to baldness, which is, unfortunately, a dominant genetic factor.* **Above:** *A pair of normal gray cockatiels, a male and a female.*

feathers, some keepers prefer to pluck the primaries. They state that it is also a painless process. This method is, however, more dangerous than wing clipping and, once again, should not be done by an amateur.

With molting, new feathers replace the clipped or plucked ones. If there is still need to restrict flight, the procedure is repeated before the bird is fully feathered and capable of flying again.

If it is given nutritious food, clean surroundings, and lots of love and attention, your pet cockatiel should be a wonderful part of your life for years to come.

Index

A lutino cockatiel (left) and a pair of normal gray cockatiels.

COCKATIELS
KW-057